WALKING TOWARD

Eternity

Making Choices For Today

SERIES TWO:
ENGAGING THE STRUGGLES OF YOUR HEART

JEFF & EMILY CAVINS

Journal

ASCENSION PRESS

West Chester, Pennsylvania

Read
Ephesians

Nihil obstat: Reverend Robert J. Pesarchick, S.T.D.
        Censor Librorum
        October 16, 2012

Imprimatur: +Most Reverend Charles J. Chaput, O.F.M. Cap.
        Archbishop of Philadelphia
        October 19, 2012

Walking Toward Eternity is a resource of *The Great Adventure* Bible Study Program.

Jeff Cavins, general editor, *The Great Adventure* Bible Study Program; co-author and presenter, *Walking Toward Eternity*
Emily Cavins, co-author, *Walking Toward Eternity*
Sarah Christmyer, editor, *The Great Adventure* Bible Study Program

Ascension Press
Post Office Box 1990
West Chester, PA 19380
Customer service: 1-800-376-0520
AscensionPress.com
WalkingTowardEternity.com

Cover design: Devin Schadt

Printed in Hong Kong

ISBN: 978-1-935940-44-9

CONTENTS

wk 1

1 - What is God Saying to you?

2 -

3 - Is there a change I need to make?

FROM THE AUTHORS

Welcome to *Walking Toward Eternity* Series Two: *Engaging the Struggles of Your Heart*. This study grew out of our desire to be more like Christ and to focus on key obstacles that hinder us from growing spiritually. Taking the time to step back and assess our lives on a topic-by-topic basis led to many moments of self-understanding, which then allowed us to turn those hurts, failures, and dead ends over to Christ to heal us. We found that the Scriptures and *Catechism* contain many answers for daily living if only we will submit ourselves to God's loving instruction. Listening and responding to God's Word is the key to the transformation we all seek.

This study is different from a typical Bible study. We have designed each lesson to use Scripture as a way to encounter Christ in meditation and prayer. As St. Augustine said, "When we pray, we speak to God; when we read the Scriptures, God speaks to us." We hope that as you study God's Word and continue this intimate conversation with him, your relationship with the Lord will deepen.

Using the Scriptures and your Journal, you will experience daily meditative prayer that will allow God's Word to work in you to instill the mind of Christ and begin to give you the grace necessary for change. Group discussion time will provide community and support, and the lectures will help focus you and challenge you to take action. Because making personal changes can be difficult on your own, these discussion groups will also keep you accountable as you follow through on the commitments you make each week.

The most dynamic aspect of this study is that each week will end with quiet time spent in the Lord's presence, where you will commit to one specific step to take in the following week. Your journal, group discussions, lectures, and actions will work together to help you identify and begin to overcome some of the obstacles that keep you from walking in the fullness of Christ: unruly appetites, shame, envy, anger, fear, loneliness, and hopelessness.

We are glad you can join us as together we engage the struggles of our hearts!

—Jeff and Emily Cavins

one

LIVING ON PURPOSE

"The heart is the place of decision, deeper than our psychic drives. It is the place of truth, where we choose life or death. It is the place of encounter ..."

— *Catechism of the Catholic Church* No. 2563

"O Lord and Master of my life!

Take from me the spirit of sloth,
faint-heartedness, lust of power, and idle talk.

But give rather the spirit of chastity (integrity),
humility, patience, and love to Thy servant.

Yea, Lord and King! Grant me to see my own errors
and not to judge my brother,
for Thou art blessed unto ages of ages. Amen."

– Lenten Prayer of St. Ephrem the Syrian[1]

Session One Outline

DVD Presentation: *"Living on Purpose"*

This video session will <u>introduce</u> the Walking Toward Eternity program, explain the various parts of the program, and share what you can expect to get out of it. Add your notes to the talk outline below:

I. **The Interior Part of Our Lives**

    A. Focus on change, personal growth

    B. Growth starts with a sober awareness of who we are

II. **How to Approach Our Struggles**

    A. Eradicate them (as in envy) or listen to and manage them:

        1. With the help of the Holy Spirit and God's Word

        2. Psalms 139:14 —"I am fearfully and wonderfully made"

    B. Ask these questions:

        1. Is God trying to say something to me?

        2. Is there a warning I need to heed?

        3. Is there a change I need to make in my life?

III. **Struggles are Normal**

IV. **Moving From "Automatic Pilot" to "On-Purpose" Living**

    A. Slow down and evaluate why we do what we do

   B. Come to know ourselves better

   C. Scrabble analogy—finding the "missing letters" in our lives

V. Hearing the Word of God

   A. Genesis 1—God spoke his Word into chaos, bringing order

   ✓ B. Matthew 11:28—God gives rest to the weary

   C. Hebrews 4:12—God's Word gives power to change

   D. James 1:22-25—God's Word is like a mirror

   E. 1 Kings 19:11-12—God speaks in a "still small voice"

   F. Isaiah 55:11—God's Word will accomplish his purpose

VI. The Need for Conversion

   A. These spiritual challenges can be controlled (Proverbs 16:32)

   B. Our goal is to become saints[2]

   C. The importance of humility—a proper assessment of who we
       are in relationship to God and others

VII. Using the *Walking Toward Eternity* Journal[3]

   A. Daily meditation (Days One–Four in Journal)

   B. *Lectio divina* ("the divine reading")

We need humility to know who we are.

1. Reading (*lectio*)

2. Meditation (*meditatio*)—in Hebrew: hagah

3. Prayer (*oratio*)

4. Contemplation (*contemplatio*)

VIII. Other Materials

A. Bible (RSV-CE or NAB)

B. *Catechism of the Catholic Church* (optional; for reference only)

C. Bookmark with steps of *lectio divina*

IX. The *Walking Toward Eternity* Process

A. Step 1: Prepare at home with *Walking Toward Eternity* Journal and Bible

B. Step 2: Participate in small-group discussion

C. Step 3: View DVD presentation

D. Step 4: In prayer, ask Jesus three questions:

1. What are you putting your hand on in my life?
   Power, load & strength

2. What specifically should I do?
   Kneel & Prayer

3. When?
   Walking in bed

X. Conclusion
while - anytime, anywhere

Group Discussion

*During this time you will get acquainted with others in your small group
and learn more about the materials and home study portion of the class.*

Small-Group Assignment

Facilitator _____

_____

Phone and/or email _____

_____

Location _____

_____

Walking Together

This study is designed to assist you in moving toward real
change in your life through prayerful daily meditation on
Scripture. The others in your small group are on the same
journey. After you have studied each topic, Jeff Cavins
will encourage you to take one concrete step to put into
practice what you have learned and create change.

Starting next week, the facilitator of your group will ask a
simple question at the beginning of each discussion time:
"Did you take the step?" A simple "yes" or "no" is all that
is needed, but you may share more as time allows.

We all know how difficult change can be. Please
remember to pray for the others in your group.

How to Use This Journal

1. Home Preparation: Days 1 to 4   *Read the text*

This journal will guide you on your daily "walk" as you prepare for the days you meet with your group. The study you do at home is less about learning than it is about hearing from God in his Word, letting that Word come into contact with your life, and responding to God in prayer. It is important to spend a small amount of time each day— fifteen to twenty minutes should be sufficient—rather than doing it all at once or at the last minute.

Four days of prayerful reading are outlined for each session. Every day, you will be prompted to think in a different way about the obstacle under discussion that week.

Day 1: <u>Meaning</u>

The first day's questions help you discover the nature of shame, anger, hopelessness, or another obstacle to your spiritual growth. Sometimes you will be asked to look up what the Bible says about the issue or provide your own observations. You may be asked to reflect on how you have struggled with the obstacle in your life. You will be provided with several Scripture verses to read and think about. Linger over this exercise, allowing the verses to penetrate your mind before recording what stands out to you.

Day 2: Importance

The second day takes this same obstacle and turns your focus to God's perspective on the issue. As in Day 1, you will be prompted to read Scripture to learn God's view on the matter. What does that obstacle look like to him? What effect does it tend to have when left unchecked? What is his answer to it? Once again, take time to savor God's Word; don't simply taste it and move on.

Day 3: Practice

The third day is similar to Days 1 and 2, but the questions build on what you have already read and ask you to consider what steps you can take to overcome this obstacle in your life. Along with the brief list of verses you are given to read carefully, you may be presented with a longer passage from the Bible that illustrates the issue or how to engage it correctly. You then will be asked to begin thinking of how your own life measures up and to decide whether something is standing in the way of change.

Day 4: Praying Scripture for a Change

After three days of thinking about the topic, Day 4 asks you to enter into a deeper, more personal encounter with the passage that has meant the most to you that week. Using *lectio divina*, you will be asked to meditate prayerfully on your chosen Scripture passage, listening to hear the voice of God speak to you and responding to him in prayer. After the group discussion and DVD presentation, you will once again pray—this time deciding on and committing to the step you will take toward change. (The instructions for *lectio divina* are on the following page.)

Optional Further Reading

Days 1 to 3 each close with a list of additional verses. These are for optional reading, if you have time and want to explore the topic more. Feel free to use a Bible concordance to find even more verses, if you desire.

Notes for Group Discussion

Space has been set aside on each day's page for discussion notes. At the top is a question that summarizes the theme for that day (for example, "What's wrong with indulging?" at the far right of Session 2, Day 1). You need not answer the question at home; it will be used later to guide group discussion of what you have gleaned during the week. The extra space will allow you to add insights you gain that day from other group members.

2. Meeting Day

Each week on your meeting day, a small group discussion and the DVD presentation will help prepare you to take the first step toward overcoming a particular obstacle. The "Meeting Day" pages of your journal are designed to help with this process.

Small-Group Discussion

To help you recall what you have been reading and thinking in regard to that week's topic, you will begin with a brief group exercise of *lectio divina* on a passage that gets to the heart of the topic. Praying with *lectio divina* in a group is a bit different than praying with it in solitude. (Directions for leading a group discussion in *lectio divina* can be found on page 10.)

The majority of the small group time will be spent discussing the insights you have gained. Four general questions are provided that summarize the goals of day. They are repeated on appropriate pages to minimize the need to flip back and forth in your journal during discussion.

Several additional questions are offered to answer if there is time remaining.

DVD Presentation

An outline of the DVD presentation is included in your journal. Feel free to take additional notes there as desired.

Quiet Time in the Lord's Presence

At the close of the DVD presentation, you will be asked to spend time in quiet prayer—before the Blessed Sacrament, if possible—asking the Lord three questions:

– What are you putting your hand on in my life?

– What specifically do you want me to do?

– When?

My Step for the Week

The last journal page for each session contains a "contract" of sorts on which you may record the specifics regarding the step you have determined to take the following week. Write it down and ask God for help as you dare to "walk the walk."

Instructions for *Lectio Divina* ("Divine Reading")

Choose a brief portion of Scripture to meditate on. Spend a few moments in a quiet place preparing your heart and asking God to meet you in his Word. Follow these steps to praying with the Scripture passage you have chosen:

1. **Read** *(Lectio):* Slowly read the verse(s), looking for details. Notice key words; verbs and nouns; and anything repeated, compared, or contrasted. What does the passage say? Write down words or phrases that stand out to you.

2. **Meditate** *(Meditatio):* Mentally "chew" on key words or images to extract their meaning. Let the words sink in and take hold. What do those words mean? Write down what you discover.

3. **Pray** *(Oratio):* Pay attention to the way your meditation connects with your life, and respond to what you find. Talk to God (not "at" him) about this.

4. **Contemplate** *(Contemplatio):* Savor being in God's presence.

5. **Resolve to Act** *(Operatio):* Make a practical resolution by which you hope to overcome the obstacle you have been reading about.

Leading a Group Exercise of *Lectio Divina*

The principles of *lectio divina* have been adapted here to help your group prepare for a fruitful discussion. You may find that people arrive to the group distracted, their minds full of cares and undone tasks. This exercise will help them slow down, set aside their concerns, and recall the Scriptures they've meditated on during the week.

A Bible passage has been carefully selected for each lesson that is rich in thoughts and images related to that topic. You will read it prayerfully as a group three times. Between readings, members of the group will speak aloud the word or phrase that stood out to them. There is no need to exhaust the passage or to get everyone to speak. Keep it simple, no more than five to ten minutes long: just enough to allow people to catch their breath and prepare their hearts.

Choose three people to read the passage out loud and respond as described below.

1. **Open with prayer.**

   Facilitator: Pray in your own words or with these: "Lord, open our minds, our ears, and our hearts, that we may be transformed by your Word." Sit still for a few minutes, quieting your hearts and preparing to hear the living Word of God, spoken to you.

2. **Read** *(Lectio):*

   Reader 1: Read the Scripture passage aloud slowly, thoughtfully.

   Group: Listen prayerfully. What did you hear? In the following silence, speak aloud the word or words that stood out to you.

3. **Meditate** *(Meditatio):*

   Reader 2: Read the same passage again, slowly.

   Group: Reflect on how Christ is speaking to you through the text. Allow his Word to speak into your heart, to touch your life. What is he saying to you? Speak it briefly into the silence that follows.

4. **Pray** *(Oratio):*

   Reader 3: Read the passage slowly a final time.

   Group: Listen quietly to God speaking to your hearts; respond silently to him. After a few minutes of silent prayer, you may share with others what is in your heart.

5. **Contemplate** *(Contemplatio):*

   Group: Spend several minutes of quiet rest in God's love.

6. **Close with the Our Father or other prayer.**

two

ENGAGING YOUR APPETITES

"Detach yourself from the goods of this world. Love and practice poverty of spirit: be content with what is sufficient for leading a simple and temperate life. Otherwise, you'll never be an apostle."

– St. Josemaría Escrivá, *The Way*

DAY 1   *Date* _____

The Problem of Uncontrolled Appetites

An appetite is a natural desire to satisfy a need. When our appetites are not controlled, they lead to things like greed; lust; overindulgence in food, drink, or things—often in an attempt to find wholeness, identity, and purpose.

Pray before you begin. Ask the Lord to help you understand why created things have such a pull on us.

1. Looking at our country and at your neighbors, what evidence of excess have you observed?   *Minimal*

2. In your experience, how do material possessions and temporal gratification correspond to happiness?
    As in all things, they can contribute to happiness when used in moderation.

3. Discover what the Bible has to say about the problem of uncontrolled appetites. Read the following verses aloud. Read each one again slowly. Repeat it in your mind and think about what it says. After each verse, write down the words, phrases, or concepts that stand out most to you.

    a. Luke 12:15   *Be on your guard against all kinds of greed.*

    b. Genesis 3:6   *good for food, pleasing to the eye, desirable for gaining wisdom*

    c. Exodus 20:17

    d. Proverbs 23:2-5

    e. Ezekiel 16:49

4. Circle the word or phrase you wrote down in Question 2 that speaks most to you. Why did you choose it?

Moderation

"What's wrong with indulging?"

5. In your life, where do you struggle with your appetites?

"Man commits idolatry whenever he honors and reveres a creature in place of God, whether this be gods or demons (for example, satanism), power, pleasure, race, ancestors, the state, money, etc. Jesus says, 'You cannot serve God and mammon.'"

– *Catechism* 2113[4]

Optional Further Reading

a. Micah 2:1-2

b. Genesis 13:2, 5-6

c. Matthew 6:24

2 Corinthians 11-3

1- John 2-15-17

DAY 2 *lust - oppose the* Date _____
will of the Father

God's Answer to Uncontrolled Appetites

Pray before you begin. Ask God to reveal to you how your appetites can be brought under the Lordship of Jesus.

1. What part does the will play when dealing with an overindulgent lifestyle?

   Concupiscence -

   Colletions v. 2

   John 6: 25-27

2. How would you define true wealth?

   Ref C C Lewis

   Ch 10 - Problem of Pain

"Those who hold goods for use and consumption
should use them with moderation, reserving the
better part for guests, for the sick and the poor."

– *Catechism* 2405[5]

---

① We are defined by our
relationship w/ God –

3. Discover what the Bible has to say about God's answer to uncontrolled appetites. Read the following verses aloud. Read each one again slowly. Repeat it in your mind, and think about what it says. After each verse, write down the words, phrases, or concepts that stand out most to you.

    a. Matthew 4:2-4

    b. 2 Timothy 1:6-7

    c. Romans 13:9

    d. Acts 20:35

    e. Acts 2:44-46   *True wealth is good works*

Matt 24

Possessions define & divide us.

Genesis 13,   *Ref Matt 19: 22*

Ref Matt 6, –Lust
Optional Further Reading   *& Matt 6 - 24*

    a. 1 Corinthians 9:24-25

Good b. Luke 12:16-23

3 Change our relationships with this word

DAY 3   *Date* _____

Engaging Your Appetites

Pray before you begin. Ask the Lord to help you gain control in the areas of your life where you struggle with your appetites.

1. According to the Bible, what can help us engage our appetites constructively? Prayerfully read these verses and meditate on them. Record your insights.

    a. 1 John 2:15-17   *- remain*

    b. Hebrews 13:5

    c. Proverbs 25:16

    d. Matthew 6:19-21

    e. 2 Timothy 2:22

2. Read the story of The Rich Young Man in Matthew 19:16-22. If the Rich Young Man had been able to do what Jesus suggested instead of holding onto his possessions, how do you think his life might have changed?

3. What might you be losing by holding onto more than you need?

> "*Temperance* is the moral virtue that moderates the attraction of pleasures and provides balance in the use of created goods."
>
> – *Catechism* 1809

Optional Further Reading

a. Romans 12:2

b. Galatians 5:16

c. Psalms 24:1

d. 1 Timothy 6:17-19

"What practical steps can lead to contentment?"

DAY 4   *Date* _____

Praying Scripture for a Change

Pray before you begin. Ask the Lord to help you face any areas of
uncontrolled appetites in your life and take a step toward change.

1. Look back through your journal for the week and select the
    Scripture passage that meant the most to you. Look it up in your
    Bible and decide whether to read it alone or in the context of the
    surrounding passage. For example, if you select Luke 12:16-23
    (which was an optional reading on Day 2), you may want to begin
    with verse 13. You can use as little as one word or phrase or as
    much as a paragraph.

Write the verse and its reference here:

2. Using the steps of *lectio divina* on page 11 or on your bookmark,
    meditate on the Scripture you chose until it turns into prayer, and
    then simply rest in the Lord, trusting that he will help you to take
    action and make a change in your life.

Read *(Lectio)*

Meditate *(Meditatio)*

"What did you
glean from your
lectio divina?"

Continued on next page …

Pray *(Oratio)*

Contemplate *(Contemplatio)*

Resolve to Act *(Operatio)*

MEETING DAY

*Date*_____

Taking the First Step

Small-Group Discussion

> *Before you begin, your group facilitator will ask, "Did you 'take the step' this week?" Only "yes" or "no" answers are necessary, but you are welcome to share your experience.*

This is the time to share the insights you received this past week and hear from the other members in the group. You will begin with a brief group exercise of lectio divina.

1. Meditate prayerfully as a group on 1 John 2:15-17. (Choose three people to look up the passage and read it aloud as described on page 10.) Take no more than five or ten minutes on this exercise.

2. Answer the following questions as a group, sharing insights gleaned from the verses you meditated on this week. (Turn back in your journal to recall what you discovered each day, and use the space provided in the margin to add new insights from the group discussion.)

    *   What's wrong with indulging? (Day 1)

    *   How does God help us with our appetites? (Day 2)

    *   What practical steps can lead to contentment? (Day 3)

    *   What did you glean from your *lectio divina?* (Day 4)

3. If there is time, continue the discussion around any of these questions:

    *   Is there a type of freedom associated with a lack of material goods? Explain your answer.

    *   How might generosity of heart help moderate our appetites?

    *   Why is it so hard to maintain self-control?

Session Two Outline

DVD Presentation: "Engaging Your Appetites"

This video session will prepare you to take the first step in engaging your appetites constructively. Add your notes to the talk outline below:

I. Introduction

II. The Garden of Eden: A Place of Moderation

    A. All things were good; not all beneficial

    B. Adam and Eve lived with eternity in their hearts (Ecclesiastes 3:11), but in a temporal world

    C. The problem of over-indulgence

    D. The choice—God's will or our will?

III. When Good Becomes Bad

    A. Genesis 3—the Fall of Adam and Eve

        1. "Forbidden fruit"—tastes and looks good, makes wise

        2. Eve indulges in something good instead of following God's will

    B. Fall results in weakened will, clouded reason, concupiscence

    C. To aim for the great (not merely good):

        1. Moderate your appetites, make good choices

        2. Love God's will over the world (1 John 2:15-17; Genesis 3:6)

            a. Lust of the flesh = "good for food"

            b. Lust of the eyes = "a delight to the eyes"

            c. Pride of life = "make one wise"

        3. Instant vs. delayed gratification (Walter Mischel marshmallow experiment)

        4. Recognize we are eternal beings; things will never satisfy

    a. St. Augustine: "Our hearts are restless until they rest in thee"

    b. Deception of the enemy—this world satisfies

    c. 2 Corinthians 11:3—don't stray from simplicity of devotion to Christ

    d. Colossians 3:2—set your minds on things above

    e. John 6:27—work for food that endures for eternal life

    f. Expectations disproportionate to possessions (Samuel Johnson)

    g. Earthly pleasures point beyond this world (C.S. Lewis)[6]

IV. Consequences of Runaway Appetites

  A. Dysfunctional relationship with God, others, and creation

  B. Possessions define and divide us

    1. Example: Jeff's library

    2. Genesis 13:6 (Lot and Abraham); Genesis 36:7 (Jacob and Esau)

  C. The warning of Solomon

V. The Cost of Over-Indulging Our Appetites

  A. Matthew 19:22—the Rich Young Man lost the joy of following Christ

  B. Genesis 3—Adam and Eve lost walking with God

  C. James 4:1-2—hurt relationships with others

  D. Matthew 6:24—we cannot serve God and mammon E. Sam's story

VI. The Solution

  A. Realize you are defined by your relationship with God

  B. Go from possessors to "wise stewards" (Matthew 24:47)

C. Hold things loosely (Luke 12:15-23)

D. Recognize what true wealth is (1 Corinthians 3:10-15)

E. Keys to combat unruly appetites:

    1. Prayer

    2. Confession

    3. Don't just resist; be obedient to Christ

    4. Commit to a life of moderation

F. Three forms of piety (Matthew 6) counter the central issues:

    1. Almsgiving—counters the lust of the eyes

        a. Exercise stewardship; divest of treasures of this world

        b. Job 31:1—make a covenant with your eyes

        c. Psalms 119:37 take custody of your eyes

    2. Prayer—counters the pride of life

    3. Fasting—counters the lust of the flesh

        a. Deuteronomy 8:3—man does not live by bread alone

        b. Catechism No. 1808 on fortitude

        c. 1 Corinthians 9:27—"I buffet my body"

        d. St. Thomas, Gregory the Great, on gluttony

        e. Ezekiel 16:49—gluttony contributed to downfall of Satan

VII. Conclusion

A. Colossians 3:1-2—"set your minds on things above"

B. Philippians 4:13—"I can do all things [through Christ] who strengthens me"

Quiet Time in the Lord's Presence

This is an opportunity for you to sit and pray silently in Christ's presence, allowing him to speak to your heart about how you can moderate your appetites in new ways. Respond by committing to a specific step you will take to bring about a needed change in your life.

Remember, mental acknowledgment that change is needed is not change. Action—responding in word and deed—is essential for lasting change.

Dear Lord,
You have already given me the greatest gift of all in your sacrifice for my sin. I owe you a debt of gratitude that I cannot repay, but I will show you my appreciation through my gratefulness for your generous provisions that have sustained me until this day. Teach me to be content with what I have and to be generous with what is really yours in the first place.

Amen.

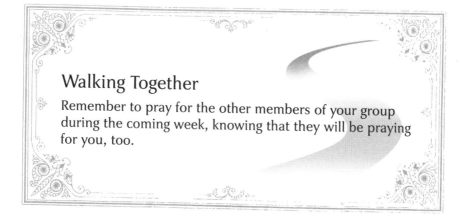

Walking Together

Remember to pray for the other members of your group during the coming week, knowing that they will be praying for you, too.

My Step for This Week ...

1. I believe the Lord is asking me to stop indulging my appetites in this situation of my life:

2. Specifically, I am going to do the following this week:

3. I will take the necessary first step on

_____.

(day and time)

three

ENGAGING YOUR SHAME

"We are not the sum of our weaknesses and failures; we are the sum of the Father's love for us and our real capacity to become the image of his Son."

– Pope John Paul II
World Youth Day 2002

DAY 1   *Date*_____

The Problem of Shame

> **Guilt is feeling bad about what you have done; shame is feeling bad about who you are.**

Pray before you begin. Ask the Lord to open your heart to hear his voice.

1. When is shame a good thing?

2. What are some causes of unhealthy shame?

3. Discover what the Bible has to say about the nature of shame. Read the following verses aloud. Read each one again slowly. Repeat it in your mind and think about what it says. After each verse, write down the words, phrases, or concepts that stand out most to you in relation to shame.

    a. Genesis 2:25

    b. Genesis 3:7, 9-10

    c. Romans 1:24-25

    d. Psalms 44:15-16

4. Recall a time when you felt ashamed. What caused it, and what impact did it have on you?

"Baptism is God's most beautiful and magnificent gift. ... We call it gift, grace, anointing, enlightenment, garment of immortality, bath of rebirth, seal, and most precious gift. It is called ... *clothing* since it veils our shame."

– *Catechism* 1216[7]

Optional Further Reading

a. Philippians 3:18-19

b. Jeremiah 3:25

c. Isaiah 45:16-17

DAY 2   *Date* _____

God's Answer to Shame

Pray before you begin. Ask the Lord to show you how he can free you from the burden of shame.

1. What have you observed to be the result of shame in people's lives?

2. Discover what the Bible has to say about God's answer to shame. Read the following verses aloud. Read each one again slowly. Repeat it in your mind and think about what it says. After each verse, write down the words, phrases, or concepts that stand out most to you.

    a. Genesis 1:27-31

    b. Romans 8:1-2

    c. Romans 8:31-39

    d. Isaiah 61:7

3. Read the story of the woman caught in adultery in John 8:3-11. What impact does Christ's action have on the shame and disgrace she must have felt?

4. As you reflect on this story and the verses in question 1, how can you better understand the depth of God's love for you? What effect does this have on the areas in your life where you experience shame?

5. Based on the verses you have been meditating on today, what answers does God have for those who feel imprisoned by shame?

Optional Further Reading

a. 2 Corinthians 5:17

b. Romans 10:11-13

c. Jeremiah 33:6-8

d. Ephesians 2:4-7

DAY 3   *Date* _____

Engaging Your Shame

Pray before you begin. Ask the Lord to help you confront your shame.

1. According to the Bible, what steps can we take to confront our
    shame? Prayerfully read these verses several times each and
    meditate on them. Record what stands out to you about living
    without shame.

    a. Psalms 119:5-7

    b. Psalms 51:5-7

    c. 2 Corinthians 7:10

    d. Philippians 3:13-14

    e. 2 Corinthians 10:3-4

2. Circle the word or phrase you wrote down in question 1.
    What is most meaningful to you? Why?

3. Read Psalms 44:15-26 several times
   through. What can you learn about what to
   do with your shame?

"What practical
steps can one take
to overcome
shame?"

Optional Further Reading

    a. 1 John 5:14-16

    b. Jeremiah 31:31-34

    c. Acts 20:32

    d. Romans 12:1-2

    e. Psalms 25:1-3

DAY 4   *Date*_____

Praying Scripture for a Change

Pray before you begin. Ask the Lord to help you face your shame and take a step toward healing.

1. Look back through your journal for the week and select the Scripture passage that meant the most to you. Look it up in your Bible and decide whether to read it alone or in the context of the surrounding passage. For example, if you select 1 John 5:14-16, you may want to begin with verse 1. You can use as little as one word or phrase or as much as a paragraph.

Write the verse and its reference here:

2. Using the steps of *lectio divina* on page 11 or on your bookmark, meditate on the Scripture you chose until it turns into prayer and then simply rest in the Lord, trusting that he will help you to take action and make a change in your life.

3. **Read** *(Lectio)*

Meditate *(Meditatio)*

"What did you glean from your *lectio divina*?"

Pray *(Oratio)*

Contemplate *(Contemplatio)*

Resolve to Act *(Operatio)*

MEETING DAY

Date _____

Taking the First Step

Small-Group Discussion

> *Before you begin, your group facilitator will ask, "Did you 'take the step' this week?" Only "yes" or "no" answers are necessary, but you are welcome to share your experience.*

This is the time to share the insights you received this past week and hear from the other members in the group. You will begin with a brief group exercise of lectio divina.

1. Meditate prayerfully as a group on Romans 8:31-39. (Choose three people to look up the passage and read it aloud as described on page 10.) Take no more than five or ten minutes on this exercise.

2. Answer the following questions as a group, sharing insights gleaned from the verses you meditated on this week. (Turn back in your journal to recall what you discovered each day, and use the space provided in the margin to add new insights from the group discussion.)

    *   Where does shame come from? (Day 1)

    *   How does God free us from unhealthy shame? (Day 2)

    *   What practical steps can one take to overcome shame? (Day 3)

    *   What did you glean from your *lectio divina?* (Day 4)

3. If there is time, continue the discussion around any of these questions:

    *   What is the difference between healthy shame and unhealthy shame?

    *   How can seeing ourselves as God sees us make a difference when we are struggling with shame?

    *   Has anyone ever said to you, "Shame on you?" How did those words impact your view of who you are?

Session Three Outline

DVD Presentation: "Engaging Your Shame"

This video session will prepare you to take the first step in engaging your shame. Add your notes to the talk outline below:

I. Introduction

    A. Good shame vs. bad shame

    B. Feeling of humiliation caused by the consequences of wrong or foolish behavior

    C. Shame versus guilt

    D. Shame associated with desire to hide or disappear

        1. Example: *The Scarlet Letter*—story of Hester Prynne

        2. Psalms 44:15-16

II. The Origins of Shame—The Fall

    A. Before the Fall, Adam and Eve "naked without shame" (Genesis 2:25)

    B. After the Fall, they covered themselves

    C. God calls Adam and Eve in Genesis 3:7-10; they hide

III. Freedom From Shame

    A. God's blessing: "be fruitful and multiply"

        1. Fruit results from God's blessing

    2. Shame runs, tries to acquire blessing by becoming fruitful

  B. Key to overcoming shame: turning to God, repentance

  C. Genesis 3:15—"protoevangelium," God gives hope

  D. The beginnings of shame

    1. Genesis 3:7, 9-10—they knew that they were naked

    2. Romans 1:24-25—exchanging the truth about God for a lie

  E. John Paul II defines shame in *Love and Responsibility*[8]

IV. Good Shame vs. Bad Shame

  A. The reason for shame

    1. Shame helps guide your conscience

    2. Shame protects your values

  B. "Good shame"

    1. You had a hand in what you did

    2. You did something that dishonored God

  C. "Bad shame"

    1. No good reason for it

      3.   For honoring God or doing something right (1 Peter 4:16)

      4.   For weakness (but: 2 Corinthians 12:9-12 "My power made perfect in weakness")

  D. Jenni's story—God can turn bad shame into an opportunity for life

V. God's Answer to Shame

  A. Revelation 12:10—Satan is our accuser

  B. Christ bore our shame and is our advocate

      1.   1 John 2:1

      2.   Matthew 27:28

      3.   Hebrews 12:2

      4.   Isaiah 50:6-9

      5.   Isaiah 53:2-7

  C. Isaiah 54: 4-5—you will forget the shame of your youth

VI. Conclusion

  A. Matthew 12:20—he will not quench a bruised reed

  B. Numbers 6:24-27—the Lord wants to lift your countenance

  C. John Paul II—"absorption of shame by love"[9]

  D. 2 Corinthians 5:17—anyone in Christ is a new creation

Quiet Time in the Lord's Presence

This is an opportunity for you to sit and pray silently in Christ's presence, allowing him to speak to your heart about how you can overcome shame in new ways. Respond by committing to a specific step you will take to bring about a needed change in your life.

Remember, mental acknowledgment that change is needed is not change. Action–responding in word and deed–is essential for lasting change.

Dear Lord,
When you created mankind in your image, you deemed it "very good." Help me to recognize that this is true today in my life, and that you see me as valuable and worthy of love just because I am. I offer you all the hurtful, negative words and deeds that have been aimed at me and which have shaped a view of myself that is contrary to yours. Take my offering and create something beautiful in me, your beloved child.

Amen.

Walking Together

Remember to pray for the other members of your group during the coming week, knowing that they will be praying

My Step for This Week …

1. I believe the Lord is asking me to walk away from shame in this situation in my life:

2. Specifically, I am going to do the following this week:

3. I will take the necessary first step on

    _____.

                        (day and time)

four

ENGAGING YOUR ENVY

"As a moth gnaws a garment, so doth envy consume a man."

– St. John Chrysostom

DAY 1   *Date* _____

The Problem of Envy

> **"Envy is a capital sin. It refers to the sadness at the sight
> of another's goods and the immoderate desire to acquire
> them for oneself, even unjustly. When it wishes grave harm
> to a neighbor it is a mortal sin ..."** – *Catechism* **2539**

Pray before you begin. Ask the Lord to open your heart to hear his voice.

1. What are some situations that cause people to struggle with envy?

2. Discover what the Bible has to say about envy. Read the following
    verses aloud. Read each one again slowly. Repeat it in your mind
    and think about what it says. After each verse, write down the
    words, phrases, or concepts that stand out most to you.

    a. James 4:1-3

    b. Genesis 30:1

    c. Proverbs 14:30

    d. James 3:14-16

3. Circle the word or phrase you wrote down in Question 2 that
    speaks most to you. Why did you choose it?

.

4. Read the story of Saul becoming jealous of David (1 Samuel 18:6-11). How did Saul act on his envy, and what was the result?

5. When you are caught up in envy, what blessing might you be missing?

Optional Further Reading

a. Proverbs 27:4

b. Ecclesiastes 4:4

c. Genesis 37:3-4

d. Matthew 27:18

DAY 2   *Date* _____

God's Answer to Envy

Pray before you begin. Ask the Lord to show you his answer to envy.

1. Think of a time when you were envious of someone else's successes, relationships, or possessions. What was the result?

2. Discover what the Bible has to say about God's answer to envy. Read the following verses aloud. Read each one again slowly. Repeat it in your mind and think about how the truth of each verse can help to overcome envy. After each verse, write down the words, phrases, or concepts that stand out most to you.

    a.   1 Timothy 6:6-8

    b.   1 Corinthians 12:26

    c.   John 21:22

"It was through the devil's envy that
death entered the world."

– Catechism 413

3. Read the story of the workers in the vineyard in Matthew 20:1-16. How does the owner respond to the workers' envy? What does this teach you about God's perspective on envy?

4. Review the key words and phrases you wrote down in Question 2. What particularly stood out to you and why?

"In the account of Abel's murder by his brother Cain, Scripture reveals the presence of anger and envy in man, consequences of original sin, from the beginning of human history."

– Catechism 2259[10]

Optional Further Reading

a. Titus 3:3-5

b. 1 Corinthians 13:4

DAY 3   *Date* _____

Engaging Your Envy

Pray before you begin. Ask the Lord to help you avoid envy.

1. According to the Bible, what practical steps can we take to keep
    from envying others? Prayerfully read these verses several times
    each and meditate on them. Record what stands out to you about
    living without envy.

    a. Galatians 5:25-26

    b. Philippians 2:3

    c. Romans 13:13

    d. Colossians 3:5, 12

2. Think of a time when you have struggled with envy. How could any
    of the verses you read in Question 1 have helped you and how?

"Envy is sadness at another's good."

– Fulton Sheen, *Victory Over Vice*

3. In 1 Corinthians 13:4-7, St. Paul describes
    some of the attributes of love. Read these
    verses and reflect on why love is the
    perfect antidote to envy.

"What practical
steps can one take
to overcome envy?"

"Envy represents a form of sadness
and therefore a refusal of charity;
the baptized person should struggle
against it by exercising good will.
Envy often comes from pride;
the baptized person should train
himself to live in humility ..."

– *Catechism* 2540

Optional Further Reading

a. Philippians 2:3-5

b. 1 Peter 2:1-3

DAY 4 *Date* _____

Praying Scripture for a Change

Pray before you begin. Ask the Lord to help you to face your envy and take a step toward healing.

1. Look back through your journal for the week and select the Scripture passage that meant the most to you. Look it up in your Bible and decide whether to read it alone or in the context of the surrounding passage. For example, if you select Philippians 2:3-5, you may want to continue through verse 9. You can use as little as one word or phrase or as much as a paragraph.

Write the verse and its reference here:

2. Using the steps of *lectio divina* on page 11 or on your bookmark, meditate on the Scripture you chose until it turns into prayer and then simply rest in the Lord, trusting that he will help you to take action and make a change in your life.

Read *(Lectio)*

Meditate *(Meditatio)*

"What did you glean
from your
lectio divina?"

Continued on next page …

Pray *(Oratio)*

Contemplate *(Contemplatio)*

Resolve to Act *(Operatio)*

MEETING DAY

Date _____

Taking the First Step

Small-Group Discussion

> *Before you begin, your group facilitator will ask, "Did you 'take the step' this week?" Only "yes" or "no" answers are necessary, but you are welcome to share your experience.*

This is the time to share the insights you received this past week and hear from the other members in the group. You will begin with a brief group exercise of lectio divina.

1. Meditate prayerfully as a group on 1 Timothy 6:3-8. (Choose three people to look up the passage and read it aloud as described on page 10.) Take no more than five or ten minutes on this exercise.

2. Answer the following questions as a group, sharing insights gleaned from the verses you meditated on this week. (Turn back in your journal to recall what you discovered each day, and use the space provided in the margin to add new insights from the group discussion.)

   • What does envy look like? (Day 1)

   • What is God's perspective on envy? (Day 2)

   • What practical steps can one take to overcome envy? (Day 3)

   • What did you glean from your *lectio divina?* (Day 4)

3. If there is time, continue the discussion around any of these questions:

   • How do feelings of entitlement lead to envy?

   • What can happen if feelings of envy go unchecked?

   • If you are struggling financially, how can you choose gratitude and contentment over envy?

Session Four Outline

DVD Presentation: "Engaging Your Envy"

This video session will prepare you to take the first step in engaging your envy. Add your notes to the talk outline below:

I. Introduction

    A. Envy is an attack on all things good

        1. St. Thomas Aquinas—envy is sorrow at another's good[11]

        2. Envy is always sinful

        3. Envy believes that when someone else wins, I lose

    B. Envy illustrated

        1. Attack on Michelangelo's David statue

        2. The Grinch (Dr. Seuss)

        3. St. John Chrysostom—envy consumes

        4. Jewish rabbinic story

    C. Envy contrasted with greed and competitiveness

        1. Greed wants what others have; envy resents the one who has

        2. Competitiveness strives to win; envy prevents others from winning

II. The Source of Envy

    A. Wisdom 2:21-24—"through the devil's envy death entered the world"

  ✓B. Galatians 5:20-23—envy vs. the fruit of the Spirit

    C. Envy roots itself in pride and flowers in hate

    D. Envy in the Bible

1. Genesis 4—Cain kills Abel

2. Genesis 37—Joseph's brothers sell him into slavery

3. 1 Samuel 18—Saul is envious of David

4. 1 Kings 3—dispute between two mothers

5. Matthew 27—the Jewish leadership hands Jesus over

6. Ralph Waldo Emerson—"Envy is the tax which all distinction must pay"

7. Romans 1:29—envy is listed among the most heinous traits

III. The Results of Envy's Poison

A. Distortion

B. Illness, sorrow (see Proverbs 14:30; Socrates)

C. Spiritual ill health

D. Counterfeit adoration (imitating Satan; "the devil's holy hour")

E. Ruined relationships

1. Envy meditates on the devil's will for someone's life and smiles

2. The antithesis of God's love, of all we're called to be

3. Archbishop Fulton Sheen—"false judgment of our own moral superiority"

4. A "de-creation" of the Body of Christ, of families

5. Example: *Amadeus* (film story of Mozart and Salieri)

F. God-given vocations are ruined (Ecclesiastes 4:4)

G. Eternal perspective narrowed to this world only

2. Tells a lie: that others' blessings diminish our good

H. Shifts focus from God's blessings to what we don't have

IV. The Remedy to Envy

A. Envy is a spiritual problem *—it is an inner*

1. Rooted in a wrong perception of and relationship with God

2. Pam's story

3. Matthew 20:1-16—"Are you envious because I'm generous?" (NAB)

B. Learn to be content (Philippians 4:11-13; 1 Timothy 6:6-8)

C. Ways to battle envy

1. Recognize envy, and call it what it is

2. Purpose to walk in love (1 Corinthians 13:4)

3. Change your focus

a. Luke 15:7—look to heavenly joy

b. Matthew 6:20—lay up treasure in heaven

c. 1 Peter 2:1-2—feed on God's Word

4. Love excellence (Philippians 4:8)

5. Don't take the bait (Philippians 1:18)

6. Make a habit of gratitude

7. Rejoice in the merits of others (Romans 12:15)

8. Express admiration

9. Walk in humility

V. Conclusion

A. Don't let even a little envy creep in (see Song of Solomon 2:15)

B. Take every thought captive to Christ (2 Corinthians 10:5)

Quiet Time in the Lord's Presence

This is an opportunity for you to sit and pray silently in Christ's presence, allowing him to speak to your heart about how you can overcome envy in new ways. Respond by committing to a specific step you will take to bring about a needed change in your life.

Remember, mental acknowledgment that change is needed is not change. Action—responding in word and deed—is essential for lasting change.

I will counter envy

> *Dear Lord,*
> *When I see others achieve, help me to rejoice. When others are rewarded, help me to commend them with sincerity. When others are chosen, help me be satisfied with what you have chosen for me. Let me learn to be content with what I have and be filled with gratitude for your provision and protection; and lead me in the path you know is best for me. I will turn my eyes to you and not to others.*
>
> *Amen.*

Envy is a distorted relationship w/ God

Walking Together

Remember to pray for the other members of your group during the coming week, knowing that they will be praying

My Step for This Week ...

1. I believe the Lord is asking me to walk away from envy in this situation in my life:

2. Specifically, I am going to do the following this week:

3. I will take the necessary first step on

    _____.

    (day and time)

five

ENGAGING YOUR ANGER

"It is better not to allow anger, however just and reasonable, to enter at all, than to admit it in ever so slight a degree; once admitted, it will not be easily expelled, for, though at first but a small plant, it will immediately grow into a large tree."

– *St. Augustine*

DAY 1   *Date* _____

The Problem of Anger

> Anger is "an emotion which is not in itself wrong, but which, when it is not controlled by reason or hardens into resentment and hate, becomes one of the seven capital sins. Christ taught that anger is an offense against the fifth commandment." – *Catechism* Glossary

Love, hate, passions cause anger

Pray before you begin. Ask the Lord to open your heart to hear his voice.

1. Can you remember a time when you had difficulty controlling your anger? What do you think was the reason?

2. Discover what the Bible has to say about anger. Read the following verses aloud. Read each one again slowly. Repeat it in your mind and think about what it says. After each verse, write down the words, phrases, or concepts that stand out most to you.

    a. Mark 7:20-23

    b. Proverbs 15:1

    c. James 4:1-2

    d. Genesis 4:4-7

"What did you learn about anger and its root?"

3. Look at the following verses. How is God's anger different than ours?

    a. Psalms 30:5

    b. Mark 3:5

    c. Psalms 86:15

"By recalling the commandment, 'You shall not kill,' our Lord asked for peace of heart and denounced murderous anger and hatred as immoral. *Anger* is a desire for revenge."

— *Catechism* 2302[13]

Optional Further Reading

    a. Proverbs 14:17

    b. Ecclesiastes 7:9

    d. Galatians 5:19-21

DAY 2   *Read Ezekiel 1-50*
                                              Date_____

God's Answer to Anger

Pray before you begin. Ask the Lord to show you the importance of engaging your anger appropriately.

1. In your experience, what are some consequences of expressing anger inappropriately?

2. Discover what the Bible has to say about anger. Read the following verses aloud. Read each one again slowly. Repeat it in your mind and think about what it says. After each verse, write down the words, phrases, or concepts that stand out most to you.

    a. Proverbs 16:32

    b. James 1:19-20   *Slow to anger*

    c. Romans 12:19

    d. Philippians 2:3

anger signals you that
something needs to be done.
anger - Not on small things -
Control on big things

3. Read Luke 22:43 and Luke 23:34.

  a. Why do you think Christ didn't respond
     with anger to his persecutors?

  b. If you were in a similar situation, how
     would you react?

Proverbs 19-11 + 15-1

"The principal passions are love
and hatred, desire and fear, joy,
sadness, and anger. In the passions, as
movements of the sensitive appetite,
there is neither moral good nor evil. But
insofar as they engage reason and will,
there is moral good or evil in them."

– *Catechism* 1772-1773

Optional Further Reading

  a. Ephesians 6:4

  b. Proverbs 15:18

Proverbs 29-11

"What are some
reasons to control
anger"

*Restrain while/until
anger - Stop, pause
get under control.
Is anger good or
bad.
options -
Take constructive action
Turn over to God.*

*forgiveness puts
anger to bed.*

*Paul
Sirach*

DAY 3   *Date*_____

Engaging Your Anger

Pray before you begin. Ask the Lord to help you confront your anger.

1. According to the Bible, what can help us overcome anger?
    Prayerfully read these verses several times each and meditate on
    them. Record what stands out to you about living without anger.

    a. James 1:19-21

    b. Ephesians 4:26-27

    c. Ephesians 4:31-32

2. Read Genesis 50:15-21. What enabled Joseph to forgive his brothers
    when he might have been angry with them for selling him into
    slavery?

3. Look again at the verses in question 1. Which of these might be
    particularly helpful in controlling anger in your life and why?

"What are some
basic principles for
controlling anger?"

4. When you are tempted to react with anger, what could you choose to express instead?

Optional Further Reading

a. Psalms 4:4 (Psalms 4:5, NAB)

b. Colossians 3:8

c. 1 Timothy 2:8

d. Psalms 37:8

e. Ephesians 4:31-32

DAY 4   *Date* _____

Praying Scripture for a Change

Pray before you begin. Ask the Lord to help you face your anger and take a step toward responding with forgiveness and humility.

1. Look back through your journal for the week and select the Scripture passage that meant the most to you. Look it up in your Bible and decide whether to read it alone or in the context of the surrounding passage. For example, if you select James 1:19-21, you may want to begin with verse 12. You can use as little as one word or phrase or as much as a paragraph.

Write the verse and its reference here:

2. Using the steps of *lectio divina* on page 11 or on your bookmark, meditate on the Scripture you chose until it turns into prayer and then simply rest in the Lord, trusting that he will help you to take action and make a change in your life.

Read *(Lectio)*

Meditate *(Meditatio)*

"What did you glean from your *lectio divina?*"

Continued on next page …

Pray *(Oratio)*

Contemplate *(Contemplatio)*

Resolve to Act *(Operatio)*

MEETING DAY

Date _____

Taking the First Step

Small-Group Discussion

> *Before you begin, your group facilitator will ask, "Did you 'take the step' this week?" Only "yes" or "no" answers are necessary, but you are welcome to share your experience.*

This is the time to share the insights you received this past week and hear from the other members in the group. You will begin with a brief group exercise of lectio divina.

1. Meditate prayerfully as a group on Ephesians 4:26-32. (Choose three people to look up the passage and read it aloud as described on page 10.) Take no more than five or ten minutes on this exercise.

2. Answer the following questions as a group, sharing insights gleaned from the verses you meditated on this week. (Turn back in your journal to recall what you discovered each day, and use the space provided in the margin to add new insights from the group discussion.)

    •   What did you learn about anger and its root? (Day 1)

    •   What are some reasons to control anger? (Day 2)

    •   What are some basic principles for controlling anger? (Day 3)

    •   What did you glean from your *lectio divina?* (Day 4)

3. If there is time, continue the discussion around any of these questions:

    •   When you were a child, how did the role models in your life handle their anger?

    •   What can happen if you suppress your anger instead of dealing with it?

    •   If you find yourself angry with someone, how do you handle it? Do you go directly to that person, or do you find yourself telling someone else about it?

    •   What types of things *should* you be angry about?

Session Five Outline

DVD Presentation: "Engaging Your Anger"

This video session will prepare you to take the first step in engaging your anger. Add your notes to the talk outline below:

I. Introduction

    A. Goal: differentiate between good and bad anger

    B. Anger does not accomplish God's righteousness (James 1:20)

    C. Repressed anger can lead to physical problems

    D. Anger leads to transgression (Proverbs 29:22)

    E. Unresolved anger can ruin your life

II. What is Anger?

    A. An emotion that rises quickly, causes a physiological reaction

    B. CCC 1772–1774

        1. Anger is one of the principal passions

        2. The passions are morally neutral

        3. The passions can be taken up in virtues or perverted in vices

III. God's Anger

    A. Jeremiah 3:12-14—at sin and injustice

    B. Ezekiel 16:26—at spiritual infidelity

    C. Jeremiah 32:30—at wrongs done

    D. John 2:14-17—Jesus and the money-changers in the Temple

IV. "Good Anger" vs. "Bad Anger"

    A. Good anger: a response to injustice or sin

        1. Ephesians 4:26—"be angry but do not sin"

     2.   Example: Candy Lightner, founder of Mothers Against Drunk Driving (MADD)

  B. Bad anger: a response to frustration, inconvenience, etc.

  C. A wrong perpetrated ("good") vs. a wrong perceived ("bad")

  D. Our job—distinguish between the two, and pause before responding

V. Anger Can Be Controlled

  A. James 1:19—be quick to hear, slow to speak, slow to anger

  B. Exodus 34:5-6—the LORD is slow to anger

  C. Ecclesiastes 7:9—do not be quickly provoked

  D. Proverbs 16:32—be slow to anger; rule your spirit

  E. Proverbs 29:11—a wise man controls anger

  F. Chad's story

VI. Practical Steps to Controlling Anger

  A. Pause; take custody of your emotions

  B. Consciously acknowledge your anger

  C. Count to ten

  D. Locate the focus of your anger

  E. Is it good or bad anger?

  F. Analyze your options—take constructive action or turn it over to God (Proverbs 19:11)

  G. Get to know your triggers

VII. Confronting an Angry Person

  A. Proverbs 15:1—"a soft answer turns away wrath"

  B. Listen to the whole story; ask clarifying questions

  C. Put yourself in the other person's shoes

  D. Share additional information

E. If you are in the wrong, confess and make restitution

VIII. Virtues to Temper Anger

A. Patience

B. Gentleness

C. Self-control

D. Forgiveness

E. Understanding

F. Winston Churchill: "A man is about as big as the things that make him angry"

G. Anne Marie's story

IX. Conclusion: Resolve to Love

Take Sirach 28:1-12 with you as you meditate and pray:

"He that takes vengeance will suffer vengeance from the Lord, and he will firmly establish his sins. Forgive your neighbor the wrong he has done, and then your sins will be pardoned when you pray. Does a man harbor anger against another, and yet seek for healing from the Lord? Does he have no mercy toward a man like himself, and yet pray for his own sins? If he himself, being flesh, maintains wrath, who will make expiation for his sins? Remember the end of your life, and cease from enmity, remember destruction and death, and be true to the commandments. Remember the commandments, and do not be angry with your neighbor; remember the covenant of the Most High, and overlook ignorance.

"Refrain from strife, and you will lessen sins; for a man given to anger will kindle strife, and a sinful man will disturb friends and inject enmity among those who are at peace. In proportion to the fuel for the fire, so will be the burning, and in proportion to the obstinacy of strife will be the burning; in proportion to the strength of the man will be his anger, and in proportion to his wealth he will heighten his wrath. A hasty quarrel kindles fire, and urgent strife sheds blood. If you blow on a spark, it will glow; if you spit on it, it will be put out; and both come out of your mouth."

Quiet Time in the Lord's Presence

*This is an opportunity for you to sit and pray silently in Christ's presence,
allowing him to speak to your heart about how you can engage your
anger in new ways. Respond by committing to a specific step you will take
to bring about a needed change in your life.*

*Remember, mental acknowledgment that change is needed is not change.
Action—responding in word and deed—is essential for lasting change.*

*Dear Lord,
Help me to express my thoughts and feelings in
a way that is pleasing to you and never hurtful
to others. When the emotion of anger rises in me,
may your Holy Spirit temper me with forgiveness,
humility, and patience, so that my words and
actions will not be ones I regret. I surrender my
will to yours and pray that I grow in charity
toward others.*

Amen.

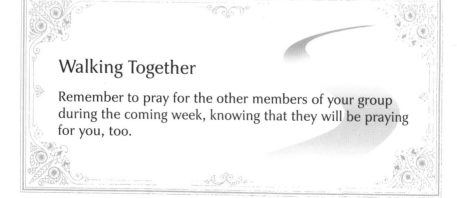

Walking Together

Remember to pray for the other members of your group
during the coming week, knowing that they will be praying
for you, too.

My Step for This Week ...

1. I believe the Lord is asking me to walk away from anger in this situation in my life:

2. Specifically, I am going to do the following this week:

3. I will take the necessary first step on

_____.

(day and time)

six

ENGAGING YOUR FEAR

"Let nothing disturb thee;
Nothing affright thee;
All things are passing;
God never changeth;
Patient endurance
Attaineth to all things;
Who God possesseth
In nothing is wanting;
Alone God suffices."

– St. Teresa of Avila

DAY 1   *Date*_____

The Problem of Fear

This lesson focuses on the fear that holds us back from walking in the freedom and love God intends for us. This fear is not to be confused with the fear of the Lord, which is a positive fear, full of awe and respect for God.

Pray before you begin. Ask the Lord to open your heart to hear his voice.

1. Look up the word "fear" in the dictionary. What does it mean, and what causes fear in people's lives?

    Don't go into the future alone.

    when fear grips you, you are not alone.

2. Discover what the Bible has to say about the nature of fear. Read the following verses aloud. Read each one again slowly. Repeat it in your mind and think about what it says. After each verse, write down the words, phrases, or concepts that stand out most to you.

    a. 1 John 4:18

        Perfect love Casts out Fear.

    b. Genesis 3:8-10

    c. Hebrews 2:14-15

    d. 2 Timothy 1:7 *God gave us a Spirit of love & power of self control.*

    ok
    Oct 26/10

    > "I ... have known a great many troubles, but most of them never happened."
    >
    > – Mark Twain

    Fear: False   *Jesus wages war on fear.*

"What is the
connection between
fear and our
relationship with
God and the devil?"

3. Circle the word or phrase you wrote down
    in Question 2 that speaks most to you.
    Why did you choose it?

4. In your life, what causes you to fear?

*we have a filial relationship
w/God.*

Ref CAT # 322 -

Genesis

"The apprehension of evil
causes hatred, aversion, and
fear of the impending evil ..."

– *Catechism* 1765

Optional Further Reading

a. Mark 4:40

b. Romans 8:15

c. Joshua 14:8

Fear brings on Amnesia.

Your fear is the Devil's Hope (Be Not afraid. Christ is risen)

DAY 2

Date _____

God's Answer to Fear

Pray before you begin. Ask the Lord to show you why it is important to overcome fear.

1. How might the fear you identified in Day 1 prohibit you from acting as you should?

    Prepare ourselves for death :

    Reward is Heaven -

    Cat : 1167

    (Take your fears to Mass (& leave there)

2. Discover what the Bible has to say about God's answer to fear. Read the following verses aloud. Read each one again slowly. Repeat it in your mind and think about what it says. After each verse, write down the words, phrases, or concepts that stand out most to you.

    a. John 14:27

    b. Romans 8:31, 35-39

    c. Isaiah 41:10

    d. Proverbs 3:25-26

"How does God
free us from fear?"

3. If you applied one of the above verses, how
    would your life be different?

"Prudent education teaches
virtue; it prevents or cures
fear ... The education of the
conscience guarantees freedom
and engenders peace of heart."

– *Catechism* 1784

Optional Further Reading

a. Luke 12:32-34

b. Hebrews 13:6

Hebrews 2: 14-15

c. Isaiah 54:14

d. Psalms 91:10-11

Rel Ps. *Ps. 34- 40*
3 2 -3   *Rev*

DAY 3   *Date*_____

Engaging Your Fear

Pray before you begin. Ask the Lord to help you stand up to your fear.

1. According to the Bible, what can help us to overcome fear?
    Prayerfully read these verses and meditate on them. Record what
    stands out to you about living without fear.

    a. Psalms 56:3-4 (Psalms 56:4-5, NAB)

    b. Ephesians 6:10-13

    c. James 4:7

    d. Philippians 4:6-7

2. Read the story of Jesus walking on the water in Matthew 14:22-32.
    How does Jesus respond to the disciples' fear? Now describe the
    difference between Peter looking at Jesus vs. looking at the wind.

"The virtue of fortitude enables one to conquer fear, even fear
of death, and to face trials and persecutions. It disposes one
even to renounce and sacrifice his life in defense of a just cause.
'The Lord is my strength and my song.'[14] 'In the world you have
tribulation; but be of good cheer, I have overcome the world.'"[15]

– *Catechism* 1808

3. What encouragement do you see in this story for facing your own fears?

> "What practical steps can be taken to overcome fear?"

4. What aspect of God's character could you focus on to help you turn away from your fear?

Optional Further Reading

a. Joshua 1:9

b. Matthew 10:31

c. Luke 12:25-28

DAY 4   *Date* _____

Praying Scripture for a Change

Pray before you begin. Ask the Lord to help you to face your fear and take a step toward healing.

1. Look back through your journal for the week and select the Scripture passage that meant the most to you. Look it up in your Bible and decide whether to read it alone or in the context of the surrounding passage. For example, if you select Ephesians 6:10-13, you may want to continue on to verse 20. You can use as little as one word or phrase or as much as a paragraph.

Write the verse and its reference here:

2. Using the steps of *lectio divina* on page 11 or on your bookmark, meditate on the Scripture you chose until it turns into prayer, and then simply rest in the Lord, trusting that he will help you to take action and make a change in your life.

Read *(Lectio)*

Meditate *(Meditatio)*

Continued on next page …

"What did you
glean from your
lectio divina?"

Pray *(Oratio)*

Contemplate *(Contemplatio)*

Resolve to Act *(Operatio)*

MEETING DAY

Date _____

Taking the First Step

Small-Group Discussion

> *Before you begin, your group facilitator will ask, "Did you 'take the step' this week?" Only "yes" or "no" answers are necessary, but you are welcome to share your experience.*

This is the time to share the insights you received this past week and hear from the other members in the group. You will begin with a brief group exercise of lectio divina.

1. Meditate prayerfully as a group on Psalms 23. (Choose three people to look up the passage and read it aloud as described on page 10.) Take no more than five or ten minutes on this exercise.

2. Answer the following questions as a group, sharing insights gleaned from the verses you meditated on this week. (Turn back in your journal to recall what you discovered each day, and use the space provided in the margin to add new insights from the group discussion.)

    *   What is the connection between fear and our relationship with God and the devil? (Day 1)

    *   How does God free us from fear? (Day 2)

    *   What practical steps can be taken to overcome fear? (Day 3)

    *   What did you glean from your *lectio divina?* (Day 4)

3. If there is time, continue the discussion around any of these questions:

    *   What is the difference between healthy fear and unhealthy fear?

    *   Can you share a real-life example of someone who overcame a particular fear?

    *   What insights did you gain about how fear may impact your life or about how it may affect others around you?

Session Six Outline

DVD Presentation: "Engaging Your Fear"

This video session will prepare you to take the first step in controlling your fear. Add your notes to the talk outline below:

I. Introduction

    A. Blessed John Paul II—"Do not be afraid! Open wide the doors to Christ."[16]

    B. Fear: False Evidence Appearing Real

II. The Problem of Fear

    A. The many words for fear

    B. Wasted hours of fear

    C. Jeff's story—debilitating fear

    D. Fear of abandonment (Matthew 8:23-26)

        1. Fear paralyzes us

        2. Fear whittles away at our confidence in God

        3. "Spiritual amnesia"

        4. Fear tells us we are alone

    E. Fear subtracts God from the future

        1. Difficulty – God = Fear

        2. Difficulty + God = Confidence and victory

    F. Spiritual battle: your fear is the devil's hope

III. Sin Contributes to the "Fear Factor"

    A. Fear will drive you away from Christ or toward him

    B. Sin is at the heart of fear (Genesis 3:8-9, Adam and Eve)

        1. Sin separates us from God

        2. Sin opens the door to fear

        3. Solution—walk again with God

IV. Jesus, The Answer to Fear—You Can Trust the Father

A. Jesus tells us, "Be not afraid!

1. Luke 1:30—angel to Mary

2. Matthew 28:5—angel to the women at the tomb

3. John 6:20—Jesus to the apostles

4. Matthew 28:10—Jesus' first words after the Resurrection

B. Jesus did not walk in fear, but in trust

C. Sarah's story

V. Keys to Conquering Fear

A. Realize who you are as a child of God

1. Slaves are fearful; sons and daughters trust

   a. CCC 322—Jesus calls us to filial trust as he showed in the desert

   b. As with Christ: Satan attempts to come between us and God

   c. Our recourse, like Christ's—knowledge of God's words and deeds

2. God is not arbitrary

3. CCC 1828—spiritual freedom of children of God

4. 1 John 4:18—"perfect love casts out fear"

5. Romans 8:15—spirit of sonship; we cry "Abba" ("Papa")

6. 1 Peter 5:7—cast your anxieties on him

B. You are not alone

1. John 14:18—"I will not leave you desolate" (NAB: "orphans")

2. Matthew 28:20—"I am with you always"

3. Joshua 1:9—the Lord is with you wherever you go

4. We walk with Emmanuel, "God with us"

5. Psalms 23:4—I fear no evil, God is with me

      6. Hebrews 13:5—God will never fail or forsake you

      7. 1 Samuel 17—David recalls God's past deeds and does not fear

C. You are loved

      1. John 3:16—God so loved the world …

      2. 2 Timothy 1:7—God did not give us a spirit of fear

      3. Psalms 23—The Lord, your shepherd

D. Be trusting in prayer

      1. CCC 2610—pray with "filial boldness"

          a. Mark 11:24

          b. Mark 9:23

      2. CCC 2734—filial trust is tested in tribulation

      3. Philippians 4:6-7—have no anxiety, but pray

      4. Jesus faced fear with prayer

      5. Psalms 34:4: seek the Lord; he will deliver you from fears

E. Confronting fear of death

      1. Hebrews 2:14-15—Jesus delivers us

      2. Revelation 1:18—Jesus holds the keys of death and Hades

      3. Archbishop Fulton Sheen quote "death can be robbed of its greatest fearfulness if we practice for it"[17]

          a. Mortification and detachment as preparation

          b. Death conquered by an affirmation of the eternal[18]

          c. Embrace the reality ("I die daily") and live in Christ

      4. CCC 1167—blessed is Sunday! (the importance of the Mass)

VI. Conclusion[19]

Quiet Time in the Lord's Presence

This is an opportunity for you to sit and pray silently in Christ's presence, allowing him to speak to your heart about how you can engage your fear in new ways. Respond by committing to a specific step you will take to bring about a needed change in your life.

Remember, mental acknowledgment that change is needed is not change. Action—responding in word and deed—is essential for lasting change.

Dear Merciful and Heavenly Father,
I recognize that there are situations in my life that I cannot resolve on my own, and for this reason, I put everything into your caring hands. I surrender to you all the adverse and negative circumstances that paralyze me. Help me to walk freely and courageously. Help me to face my fears and take the necessary steps to overcome them with your grace.

Amen.

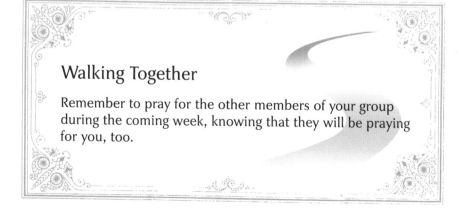

Walking Together

Remember to pray for the other members of your group during the coming week, knowing that they will be praying for you, too.

My Step for This Week …

1. I believe the Lord is asking me to walk away from fear in this situation in my life:

2. Specifically, I am going to do the following this week:

3. I will take the necessary first step on

    _____.

    (day and time)

seven

ENGAGING YOUR LONELINESS

"We have all known the long loneliness, and we have learned that the only solution is love and that love comes with community."

– Dorothy Day

DAY 1   *Date* _____

The Problem of Loneliness

Pray before you begin. Ask the Lord to open your heart to hear his voice.

1. When you think of a lonely person, what comes to mind? Describe some things that lead to loneliness in our society.

2. Discover what the Bible has to say about loneliness. Read the following verses aloud. Read each one again slowly. Repeat it in your mind and think about what it says in relation to loneliness. After each verse, write down the words, phrases, or concepts that stand out most to you.

    a. Genesis 2:18

    b. 1 Corinthians 12:24-27

    c. Psalms 142:4

    d. Ecclesiastes 4:7-12

"In the West there is loneliness, which I call the leprosy of the West. In many ways it is worse than our poor in Calcutta."

— Blessed Teresa of Calcutta

3. What is the difference between being alone and feeling lonely?

"The human person needs to live in society. ... Through the exchange with others, mutual service and dialogue with his brethren, man develops his potential; he thus responds to his vocation."

– *Catechism* 1879[20]

Optional Further Reading

a. Psalms 102:7-10

b. Psalms 38:11

c. 2 Timothy 4:16

d. Psalms 25:16

DAY 2   *Date*_____

God's Answer to Loneliness

Pray before you begin. Ask the Lord to show you his antidote to loneliness.

1. What are some ways that people try to escape their loneliness?

2. Discover what the Bible has to say about God's answer to loneliness. Read the following verses aloud. Read each one again slowly. Repeat it in your mind and think about what it says. After each verse, write down the words, phrases, or concepts that stand out most to you.

    a. Genesis 2:18

    b. Exodus 25:8

    c. Psalms 68:5-6

    d. Matthew 1:23

    e. Matthew 28:20

    f. Matthew 19:29

"What are some of the ways God frees us from loneliness?"

3. Circle the word or phrase you wrote down in Question 2 that speaks most to you. Why did you choose it?

4. What are some tangible ways that God is with you?

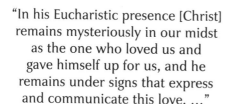

"In his Eucharistic presence [Christ] remains mysteriously in our midst as the one who loved us and gave himself up for us, and he remains under signs that express and communicate this love. ..."

– *Catechism* 1380[21]

Optional Further Reading

a. Genesis 28:15

b. Deuteronomy 31:8

c. Isaiah 43:2

d. Hebrews 13:5

e. Isaiah 41:10

DAY 3   *Date*_____

Engaging Your Loneliness

Pray before you begin. Ask the Lord to help you confront your loneliness.

1. According to the Bible, what practical steps can we take to
    overcome loneliness? Prayerfully read these verses several times
    each and meditate on them. Record what stands out to you about
    living without loneliness.

    a. James 4:8

    b. Romans 12:9

    c. Hebrews 10:24-25

    d. 1 Timothy 5:5

    e. Psalms 25:16

2. Read about Job's situation in Job 19:13-27. What caused Job to feel
    abandoned and lonely? How was he able to overcome this?

"What positive steps can help overcome loneliness?"

3. As you reflect on this story and the verses in question 2, what positive steps can you take to walk away from loneliness?

4. How could reaching out to someone else help one to overcome loneliness?

Optional Further Reading

a. Mark 15:33-34

b. Psalms 73:25-26

c. 1 Corinthians 12:24-27

d. Proverbs 18:24

DAY 4   *Date* _____

Praying Scripture for a Change

Pray before you begin. Ask the Lord to help you turn away from your loneliness and take a step toward reaching out to someone else.

1. Look back through your journal for the week and select the Scripture passage that meant the most to you. Look it up in your Bible and decide whether to read it alone or in the context of the surrounding passage. For example, if you select Mark 15:33-34, you may want to continue reading to verse 40. You can use as little as one word or phrase or as much as a paragraph.

Write the verse and its reference here:

2. Using the steps of *lectio divina* on page 11 or on your bookmark, meditate on the Scripture you chose until it turns into prayer and then simply rest in the Lord, trusting that he will help you to take action and make a change in your life.

Read *(Lectio)*

Meditate *(Meditatio)*

Continued on next page ...

"What did you
glean from your
lectio divina?"

Pray *(Oratio)*

Contemplate *(Contemplatio)*

Resolve to Act *(Operatio)*

MEETING DAY   *Date*_____

Taking the First Step

Small-Group Discussion

> *Before you begin, your group facilitator will ask, "Did you 'take the step' this week?" Only "yes" or "no" answers are necessary, but you are welcome to share your experience.*

This is the time to share the insights you received this past week and hear from the other members in the group. You will begin with a brief group exercise of lectio divina.

1. Meditate prayerfully as a group on Psalms 139:1-18. (Choose three people to look up the passage and read it aloud as described on page 10.) Take no more than five or ten minutes on this exercise.

2. Answer the following questions as a group, sharing insights gleaned from the verses you meditated on this week. (Turn back in your journal to recall what you discovered each day, and use the space provided in the margin to add new insights from the group discussion.)

    •   What is loneliness? (Day 1)

    •   What are some of the ways God frees us from loneliness? (Day 2)

    •   What positive steps can help overcome loneliness? (Day 3)

    •   What did you glean from your *lectio divina?* (Day 4)

3. If there is time, continue the discussion around any of these questions:

    •   How would you describe the difference between solitude and loneliness?

    •   Can you think of a time when you reached out to someone else even though you felt lonely? What was the result?

    •   What are some ways to find new friends if your old friends have changed or you have moved to a new location?

    •   Do you think social media helps alleviate loneliness or increases it?

Session Seven Outline

DVD Presentation: "Engaging Your Loneliness"

This video session will prepare you to take the first step in overcoming loneliness. Add your notes to the talk outline below:

I. Introduction

    A. Illustration (*Cipher in the Snow* by Jean Mizer)

    B. Being disconnected from others; lack of interaction

    C. Mother Teresa on loneliness, the "leprosy of the West"

    D. AARP survey—35 percent of adults over 40 are chronically lonely[22]

II. Causes of Loneliness

    A. Rootlessness

    B. Restlessness

    C. Fantasy

    D. Alienation (Beatrice's story)

    E. Depression

III. Reasons for Loneliness

   A. Examples

   B. Sin, the "prime alienator"

     1. Destroys love and trust

     2. Weakens or destroys relationship with God

     3. Breaks harmony with others

     4. Stems from the Fall (Genesis 3:7-9, 24)

     5. As it relates to sin: a precursor of hell (absence of God's presence)

   C. The ever-changing character of things

     1. Ecclesiastes 1:2-11—vanity of vanities

     2. Hebrews 13:14—"here we have no lasting city"

     3. Rabbinic story (Hofetz Chaim)—we are passing through

   D. Technology

   E. The nature of the human person (see Ecclesiastes 6:7)

IV. God's Answer to Loneliness

    A. Old Testament—God dwelt with his people

    B. New Testament—Emmanuel, "God with us"

    C. God takes on our loneliness (Garden of Gethsemane; on the cross)

    D. Matthew 28:20—"I will be with you always"

    E. God gives us the Church (see Psalms 68:5-6; Psalms 68:6-7, NAB)

V. Dealing With Loneliness

    A. Move away from sin and toward the kingdom

        1. Repent

        2. Move toward the kingdom (meditate on Matthew 5–7)

    B. Run to Jesus

    C. Be a friend

    D. Cultivate a few strong relationships (Proverbs 18:24)

VI. Not Struggling With Loneliness? Look Out for Lonely People

Quiet Time in the Lord's Presence

This is an opportunity for you to sit and pray silently in Christ's presence, allowing him to speak to your heart about how you can engage loneliness in new ways. Respond by committing to a specific step you will take to bring about a needed change in your life.

Remember, mental acknowledgment that change is needed is not change. Action – responding in word and deed – is essential for lasting change.

> *Dear Lord,*
> *Through your mercy, I cling to your promise that you will not leave me or forsake me. Let me feel your presence when I am alone and when I am among others. When I see those who are isolated, abandoned, or alone, let me be your hands to reach out to them. You are my spouse and my comfort in all situations, and your Holy Spirit can ultimately fill any hole in my heart.*
>
> *Amen.*

Walking Together

Remember to pray for the other members of your group during the coming week, knowing that they will be praying for you, too.

My Step for This Week ...

1. I believe the Lord is asking me to walk away from loneliness in this situation in my life:

2. Specifically, I am going to do the following this week:

3. I will take the necessary first step on

    _____.

    (day and time)

eight

ENGAGING YOUR HOPELESSNESS

"[A] person whose head is bowed and whose eyes are heavy cannot look at the light."

– Christine de Pizan, *Ditié de Jehanne d'Arc*

DAY 1   *Date*_____

The Problem of Hopelessness

Pray before you begin. Ask the Lord to open your heart to hear his voice.

1. Look up the word "hopelessness" in the dictionary. How is
    hopelessness defined?

2. Discover what the Bible has to say about hopelessness and despair.
    Read the following verses aloud. Read each one again slowly. Repeat
    it in your mind and think about what it says. After each verse, write
    down the words, phrases, or concepts that stand out most to you.

    a. Lamentations 3:17-18

    b. Job 7:6-7

    c. Ecclesiastes 2:20-21

    d. Ephesians 2:12

"In an age of hope men looked up at the night sky and saw 'the
heavens.' In an age of hopelessness they call it simply 'space.'"

– Peter Kreeft

3. Think of a time in your life when you felt hopeless. What caused you to feel this way?

4. How can feelings of hopelessness turn into despair?

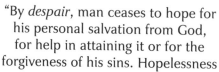

"By *despair*, man ceases to hope for his personal salvation from God, for help in attaining it or for the forgiveness of his sins. Hopelessness is contrary to God's goodness, to his justice–for the Lord is faithful to his promises–and to his mercy."

– *Catechism* 2091

Optional Further Reading

a. Psalms 69:20

b. Ezekiel 7:27

c. Psalms 33:17

DAY 2   *Date* _____

God's Answer to Hopelessness

Pray before you begin. Ask the Lord to show you the antidote to hopelessness.

1. Recall a time when you felt hopeless. Write a brief prayer that expresses how you felt.

2. Discover what the Bible has to say about God's answer to hopelessness. Read the following verses aloud. Read each one again slowly. Repeat it in your mind and think about what it says. After each verse, write down the words, phrases, or concepts that stand out most to you.

    a. Jeremiah 29:11

    b. Romans 5:1-2, 5

    c. Romans 15:4

    d. Titus 2:11-14

3. Circle the word or phrase you wrote down in Question 2 that speaks most to you. Why did you choose it?

4. How can our actions of love bring hope to others?

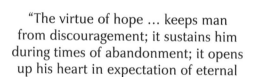

"The virtue of hope ... keeps man from discouragement; it sustains him during times of abandonment; it opens up his heart in expectation of eternal beatitude."

– *Catechism* 1818

Optional Further Reading

a. Hosea 2:15

b. 2 Corinthians 4:8-10

c. Romans 8:24

d. Psalms 9:18

DAY 3   *Date* _____

Engaging Your Hopelessness

Pray before you begin. Ask the Lord to help you find hope in him.

1. According to the Bible, how can we overcome hopelessness?
    Prayerfully read these verses several times each and meditate
    on them. Record what stands out to you about living without
    hopelessness.

    a. Psalms 33:18-23

    b. Psalms 42:5-6

    c. Ecclesiastes 9:4

    d. 2 Corinthians 4:16-18

2. Read the story of the two disciples walking to Emmaus in Luke
    24:13-35. What might have tempted them to lose hope? How did
    Jesus help them to overcome this?

*"A man devoid of hope and conscious of being
so has ceased to belong to the future."*

– Albert Camus

3. As you reflect on this story and the verses in question 1, what positive steps can you take to overcome feeling of hopelessness?

"What positive steps can you take to overcome hopelessness?"

Optional Further Reading

a. Psalms 25:15

b. Romans 4:18

c. Proverbs 24:14

d. Acts 27:20-25

e. 2 Corinthians 4:1

DAY 4   *Date*_____

Praying Scripture for a Change

Pray before you begin. Ask the Lord to help you turn away from hopelessness and despair and take a step toward healing.

1. Look back through your journal for the week and select the Scripture passage that meant the most to you. Look it up in your Bible and decide whether to read it alone or in the context of the surrounding passage. For example, if you select 2 Corinthians 4:16-18, you may want to begin with verse 1. You can use as little as one word or phrase or as much as a paragraph.

Write the verse and its reference here:

2. Using the steps of *lectio divina* on page 11 or on your bookmark, meditate on the Scripture you chose until it turns into prayer and then simply rest in the Lord, trusting that he will help you to take action and make a change in your life.

Read *(Lectio)*

Meditate *(Meditatio)*

"What did you glean from your *lectio divina?*"

Continued on next page …

Pray *(Oratio)*

Contemplate *(Contemplatio)*

Resolve to Act *(Operatio)*

MEETING DAY   *Date*_____

Taking the First Step

Small-Group Discussion

> *Before you begin, your group facilitator will ask, "Did you 'take the step' this week?" Only "yes" or "no" answers are necessary, but you are welcome to share your experience.*

This is the time to share the insights you received this past week and hear from the other members in the group. You will begin with a brief group exercise of lectio divina.

1. Meditate prayerfully as a group on Romans 8:31-35. (Choose three people to look up the passage and read it aloud as described on page 10.) Take no more than five or ten minutes on this exercise.

2. Answer the following questions as a group, sharing insights gleaned from the verses you meditated on this week. (Turn back in your journal to recall what you discovered each day, and use the space provided in the margin to add new insights from the group discussion.)

    • What is at the root of feeling hopeless? (Day 1)

    • What does God offer us in place of hopelessness and despair? (Day 2)

    • What positive steps can you take to overcome hopelessness? (Day 3)

    • What did you glean from your *lectio divina?* (Day 4)

3. If there is time, continue the discussion around any of these questions:

    • How can we prevent our lack of hope from turning into despair?

    • What are some ways you can help someone who feels all is hopeless, especially those who have lost loved ones?

    • How can you stay hopeful in the face of failure?

    • Is your hope solidly in God, or is it in something else?

Session Eight Outline

DVD Presentation: "Engaging Your Hopelessness"
This video session will prepare you to take the first step in overcoming hopelessness. Add your notes to the talk outline below:

I. **Introduction**

II. **Examples of Hopelessness**

    A. Job 7:5-7

    B. Jonah 4:3

    C. Psalms 69:20

III. **Causes of Hopelessness**

IV. **Hope: A Theological Virtue**

    A. Infused at baptism

    B. Hope can grow (See CCC 1266)

    C. CCC 2090—"the confident expectation of divine blessing and the beatific vision of God"

    D. CCC 2091—the first commandment is concerned with sins against hope: despair and presumption

V. **The Biblical View of Hope**

    A. Based on God's power and knowledge (contrast Plato: hope limited to subjective perspective)

    B. Hope is certain

    C. *Tikva*, "hope"

D. Ecclesiastes 9:4—as long as there is life, there is hope

E. Hopelessness is when God is lost as point of reference

VI. The World's View of Hope
A. Nietzsche—hope is the worst of evils

B. Contrary to biblical view: hope deferred makes the heart sick

VII. Hope: A Guiding Principle
A. Examples of hope in spite of failure (Abraham Lincoln)

B. Hope is a crossroad in life—can guide or lead astray

C. The course the heart sets when given a vision

D. Jeff's fishing story (hope based on the Father's Word)

VIII. Misplaced Hopes
A. In riches (1 Timothy 6:17)

B. In other people (Psalms 118:8) — *Read in Bible*

C. In idols (Jeremiah 14:22)

D. In things (Psalms 33:17)

IX. God Wants Us to Have Hope
A. Hosea 2:14-15: the Valley of Achor ("trouble") is made a door of hope

X. What to Do in Times of Hopelessness *Read*
A. Cry out to God (Psalms 119:147)

    1. Jeannie's story

    2. 1 Timothy 5:5—put your hope in God

    3. Hebrews 6:19—"behind the curtain," an anchor for the soul

    4. Isaiah 40:28-31—hope in the LORD = renewed strength

  B. Take stock of where you are putting your hope

  C. Put your hope in God

  D. Put your hope in his Word

    1. Psalms 130:5

    2. Romans 15:4

    3. Psalms 33:18

  E. Take Christ's yoke upon yourself

    1. Matthew 11:29

    2. Hosea 4:12

  F. Don't rely on your own understanding (Proverbs 3:5-6)

  G. Take responsibility for your moods (Ex: 1 Samuel 30:1-6)

  H. Three lessons from Israel's return from exile:

    1. They rebuilt the Temple: engage in the sacraments, Mass

    2. They read from the Law: read God's Word

    3. They rebuilt the walls: become a part of the community

XI. God Has Plans to Give You Hope

  A. Jeremiah 29:11

  B. Cindy's story

Quiet Time in the Lord's Presence

This is an opportunity for you to sit and pray silently in Christ's presence, allowing him to speak to your heart about how you can overcome hopelessness in new ways. Respond by committing to a specific step you will take to bring about a needed change in your life.

Remember, mental acknowledgment that change is needed is not change. Action—responding in word and deed—is essential for lasting change.

> *Dear Lord,*
> *Let me see through your eyes the goodness in this world and in others. Fill me with your hope and consolation, so that I may face tomorrow with the desire to persevere and be a light where darkness hides the truth of your goodness. Open my eyes to the light of hope, giving me a fresh look at what is real and true. You are the Way, the Truth, and the Life. I commit to following you.*
> *Amen.*

See 1 Tim 18

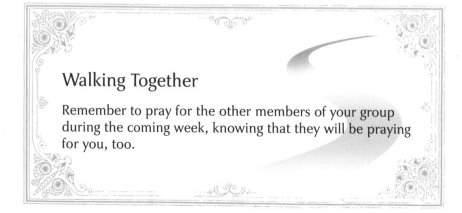

Walking Together

Remember to pray for the other members of your group during the coming week, knowing that they will be praying for you, too.

My Step for This Week ...

1. I believe the Lord is asking me to walk away from hopelessness in this situation in my life:

2. Specifically, I am going to do the following this week:

3. I will take the necessary first step on

_____.

(day and time)

Endnotes

1. As quoted by goarch.org/resources/prayers/saint_ephrem.

2. See the Vatican II document, *Lumen gentium* (Dogmatic Constitution on the Church) ch. 5: "The Universal Call to Holiness."

3. Home preparation for each day is explained in the *Walking Toward Eternity* Journal, pages 9-10. Instructions for *lectio divina* follow on pages 11-12.

4. Matthew 6:24.

5. St. Gregory of Nazianzus, *Oratio* 40, 3-4: PG 36, 361C.

6. C.S. Lewis, Pte. Ltd. *The Problem of Pain*. New York: HarperCollins, 1940, 1996.

7. See Genesis 4:8-12.

8. Karol Wojtyla (Blessed John Paul II), *Love and Responsibility* (San Francisco: Ignatius Press, 1993), 194.

9. Wojtyla, *Love and Responsibility*, 181.

10. See Genesis 4:8-12.

11. Thomas Aquinas, *Summa Theologica*, II-II, 36, 2.

12. Fulton Sheen, *Victory Over Vice*, 20.

13. Matthew 5:21.

14. Psalms 118:14.

15. John 16:33.

16. From the opening Mass of Blessed Pope John Paul II's pontificate, October 22, 1978.

17. Fulton Sheen, *Peace of Soul*, Liguori, MD: Liguori, 1996), 227.

18. Sheen, *Peace of Soul*, 228.

19. Illustration from C.S. Lewis, *Prince Caspian: The Return to Narnia, The Chronicles of Narnia* (1951), 141.

20. See *Gaudium et spes* 25 § 1.

21. See Galatians 2:20.

22. As reported in *Atlantic Magazine*, May 2012, "Is Facebook Making Us Lonely?"

Bibliography

Augustine, St. *The Teachings of the Saints in Their Own Words* by a Parish Priest, taken from *The Catholic Church the Teacher of Mankind, Vol 3*. New York: Office of Catholic Publications, 1905.

Camus, Albert. *The Myth of Sisyphus, and Other Essays*. New York: Vintage Books, 1991.

Chrysostom, St. John. As quoted in Wilstach, Frank Jenners. *A Dictionary of Similes*. Boston: Little, Brown, and Company, 1916.

Day, Dorothy. *The Long Loneliness*. New York: Harper Collins, 1952.

de Pizan, Christine. *Ditie de Jehanne d'Arc*. Society for the Study of Medieval Languages and Literature, 1977.

de Sales, St. Francis. *Introduction to the Devout Life*. Charlotte, NC: Saint Benedict Press, 1994.

Ephrem, St. "Lenten Prayer" as quoted by www.goarch.org/resources/prayers/saint_ephrem.

Escrivá, Josemaría. *The Way*. New York: Image Books, 1982,

John Paul II, Blessed. 17th World Youth Day, Solemn Mass, Toronto, July 28, 2002.

Kreeft, Peter. As quoted by catholiceducation.org/articles/apologetics/ap0018.html.

Lewis, C.S., *The Problem of Pain*. New York: HarperCollins, 1940, 1996.

Sheen, Fulton J. *Peace of Soul*. Liguori, Missouri: Liguori Publications, 1996.

Sheen, Fulton J. *Victory over Vice*. New York: P.J. Kenedy & Sons, 1939.

Teresa of Avila, St. *Let Nothing Disturb You*. Notre Dame, IN: Ave Maria, 2008.

Teresa of Calcutta. *A Simple Path*. New York: Ballantine, 1995.

Teresa of Calcutta. *Commonweal*. December 19, 1997.

Twain, Mark; Holms, John P.; Baji, Karin. *Bite-Size Twain: Wit and Wisdom from the Literary Legend*. New York: St. Martin's Press. 1998.

Wojtyla, Karol. *Love and Responsibility*. San Francisco: Ignatius, 1993.